sing Psalms!

MELODY EDITION

First published in Great Britain by the
BRITISH & FOREIGN BIBLE SOCIETY, Stonehill Green, Westlea, Swindon,
SN5 7DG

Bible text is reproduced from the Good News Bible © American Bible Society, New
York, 1966, 1971 and 4th edition 1976, published by The Bible Societies/Harper
Collins, with permission.

ISBN 0564 081159

Cover design by Jane Taylor
Music processed by MSS Studios, Cae Deintur, Dolgellau, Gwynedd
Printed and Bound in Great Britain by BPCC Wheatons Ltd, Exeter

CONTENTS

Title	Composer	Psalm	No
I call to the Lord for help	Christopher Norton	3	1
When I lie down	Norman Warren	4	2
Answer me	Christopher Norton	4	3
Listen to my words, O Lord	Christopher Norton	5	4
Listen to my words, O Lord	Norman Warren	5	5
O Lord, our Lord	David French	8	6
Sing praise to the Lord	Bob Fraser	9	7
How much longer?	Philip Warren	13	8
I will sing to you	Sheena Peckham	13	9
Lord, who may enter	Bob Fraser	15	10
I love you, O Lord	John Pantry	18	11
The Law of the Lord	Christopher Norton	19	12
The heavens declare	Bob Fraser	19	13
The Lord is my shepherd	Norman Warren	23	14
Fling wide the gates	Norman Warren	24	15
Fling wide the gates	Bob Fraser	24	16
Fling wide the gates	Derek Howell	24	17
Teach me your ways	Eric Hewitt	25	18
The Lord is my light	Philip Warren	27	19
The Lord is my light	Sarah Lacy	27	20
Have faith	Bob Fraser	27	21
Ascribe to the Lord	Bob Fraser	29	22
Praise the Lord	Derek Howell	29	23
Lord, your constant love	Norman Warren	36	24
Lord, you put a new song	Bob Fraser	40	25
May the Lord	Bob Fraser	42	26
There is a river	Bob Fraser	46	27
Clap your hands	Norman Warren	47	28
Create in me	Christopher Norton	51	29
The sacrifices of God	Bob Fraser	51	30
I will give you thanks	Norman Warren	63	31
Everything shouts	Norman Warren	65	32
May the people praise you	Norman Warren	67	33
Praise the Lord	John Barnard	68	34
Praise the Lord	Norman Warren	72	35
May he endure	John Pantry	72	36
Start the music	Derek Howell	81	37
Almighty God	Bob Fraser	84	38
How good it is	Richard Pain	92	39
The Lord is king	Norman Warren	93	40
Come, let us bow down	Bob Fraser	95	41

Come, let us praise	*Bob Fraser*	95	42
Sing a new song	*Norman Warren*	98	43
Shout for joy to the Lord	*Norman Warren*	100	44
Sing to the Lord	*Norman Warren*	100	45
Sing to the Lord	*Philip Warren*	100	46
Praise the Lord, O my soul	*Norman Warren*	104	47
From the east	*Bob Fraser*	113	48
Not to us	*Bob Fraser*	115	49
Praise, praise the Lord	*Paul Herrington*	117	50
Steadfast love	*Bob Fraser*	118	51
Your word, O Lord	*Christopher Norton*	119	52
Show me	*Roger Mayor*	119	53
Happy are those	*Eric Hewitt*	119	54
I was glad	*Norman Warren*	122	55
Lord, I look up to you	*Norman Warren*	123	56
What if the Lord?	*Norman Warren*	124	57
When the Lord brought us back	*Norman Warren*	126	58
Unless the Lord	*Andrew Maries*	127	59
O Israel put your hope	*Bob Fraser*	130	60
Out of the depths	*Andrew Maries*	130	61
A prayer of humble trust	*Norman Warren*	131	62
How good and pleasant	*Bob Fraser*	133	63
Come, praise the Lord	*Don Scully*	134	64
Come, praise the Lord	*Bob Fraser*	134	65
By the rivers of Babylon	*Bob Fraser*	137	66
By the waters of Babylon	*Andrew Maries*	137	67
I will praise you	*Bob Fraser*	138	68
Praise the Lord	*Norman Warren*	146	69
Praise the Lord	*Norman Warren*	148	70
Praise the Lord	*Norman Warren*	149	71
Praise God in his temple	*C V Stanford*	150	72
Praise the Lord	*Lee Abbey*	150	73
Praise God in his temple	*Derek Howell*	150	74

FOREWORD

by Bishop Colin Buchanan

What can you do with the Psalms nowadays? Well, you can omit them – or you can say them; you can give a complex setting to a cathedral choir and ask the congregation to remain silent throughout; or you can have another go at singing them congregationally, and, once you've tried Anglican chant, you can have a go at something metrical, or a Grail setting with a cantor and congregational antiphons – or you can try the odd psalm cut to the shape of a charismatic chorus. Many churches, however, conclude that it's all too difficult, and there's a strong temptation to say that no psalm-singing is better than bad psalm-singing.

Yet when a church concludes that the Psalms are too difficult, then it is that church which loses out; for the major song-book of the Bible is being set aside and deemed unable to contribute to our worship today. The task is admittedly often made harder by ancient versions of the scriptures, by lack of pointing, by little teaching, and by little apparent cohesion with the rest of the service. If the lead given by choir and instruments is weak or indistinct, then the frustration is great.

Sing Psalms! is a new concept, using modern versions of scripture, covering a good selection of Psalms, without a relentless insistence on the lot. The music reaches delightful heights, and is within the range of congregations which are ready to learn. Everyone involved in leading music in churches should have a copy, and I shall hope to find myself singing from it as I go on my rounds. Indeed, I would judge that in some churches this format is exactly the best way to ensure that some high peaks of scripture in song still occupy the landscape of our worship.

June 1991

Colin Buchanan

Sing Psalms!

1. I Call To The Lord For Help

Psalm 3

CHRISTOPHER NORTON

ANTIPHON (All)

Moderato

I call to the Lord for help, and from his sac - red

hill he an - swers me.

me. ——— He an - swers me.

* Optional harmony for Choir

Solo or Choir

You, O Lord, are al - ways my shield from dan - ger; you give me vic - to -

ry ——— and re - store my cour - age.

Solo or Choir

I lie down and sleep, and all night long the Lord pro - tects — me; the

Lord pro - tects me.

Solo or Choir

Vic - to - ry comes from the Lord may he bless his peo - ple; — may he

bless his peo - ple.

2. When I Lie Down

Psalm 4

NORMAN WARREN

ANTIPHON (All)

Gently

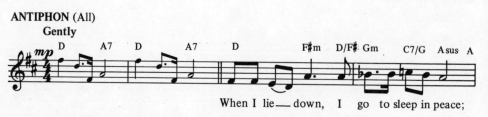

When I lie— down, I go to sleep in peace;

You a-lone, O Lord, keep me per - fect-ly safe.

An-swer me when I pray   oh God, my de-fen-der, When I was in tro-uble you helped me, be

kind   to me now   and hear my prayer.

There are ma-ny who pray___   give us more bless-ings, O Lord,   look on us with kind-ness.

But   the joy that you have gi-ven me ___ is more than they will ev-er have. ___ with

all their corn and wine.

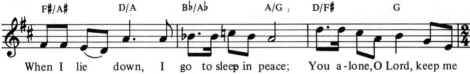

When I lie down, I go to sleep in peace; You a-lone, O Lord, keep me

per - fect - ly safe.

3. Answer Me

CHRISTOPHER NORTON

Psalm 4

ANTIPHON (All)

An-swer me when I pray, O God, my de-fen-der, An-swer me,

when I pray, O God my de-fen-der.

Choir (or Solo) to ANTIPHON

When I was in trou-ble you helped me. Be kind to me now and hear my prayer.

CHOIR (or Solo)
Slower

When I lie down, — I go to sleep in peace. You a-lone, O Lord, keep me

per-fect-ly safe.

4. Listen To My Words, O Lord

Psalm 5

CHRISTOPHER NORTON

ANTIPHON
Broadly

Lis - ten to my words, O Lord, and — hear my sighs;

Lis - ten to my — cries for help, my God — and my King.

CHOIR

I pray to you, O Lord; You hear my voice in the morn-ing; at

to ANTIPHON

sun - rise I off - er my prayer and wait — for your an - swer.

CHOIR

You are not a God who is pleased with wrong - do - ing; you al -

to ANTIPHON

low no ev - il in your pres-ence.

CHOIR

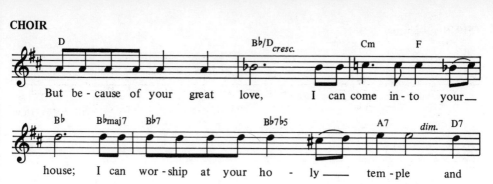

But be-cause of your great love, I can come in-to your— house; I can wor-ship at your ho-ly —— tem-ple and bow down to you in rev'- rence.

5. Listen To My Words, O Lord

Psalm 5

NORMAN WARREN

ANTIPHON (Choir or all)

Lis-ten to my words, O Lord and hear my sighs.

Lis-ten to my cries for help, my God and King. *Fine*

Solo

I pray to you, O Lord, you hear my voice in the mor-ning; At

sun-rise I of-fer my prayer and wait for your an-swer.

Solo

Be - cause of your great love I can come in - to your house.___ I can

to ANTIPHON

wor - ship in your ho - ly tem - ple and bow down to you in rev - erence.

6. O Lord Our Lord

Psalm 8

DAVID FRENCH

Lively

ALL

O Lord, our___ Lord, ___

___ your great- ness is seen in all the world. O Lord our___ Lord, ___

last time to ⊕ Coda

___ your great - ness is seen in all the world. ___

MEN

Your___ praise rea-ches up___ to the hea-vens, _____ it is sung by chil - dren and

LADIES

Your praise rea-ches up___ to the hea-vens, _____ it is

MEN

ba - bies, _____ You are safe and se-cure from all your en - e - mies

LADIES

sung by chil - dren and ba - bies _____ You are

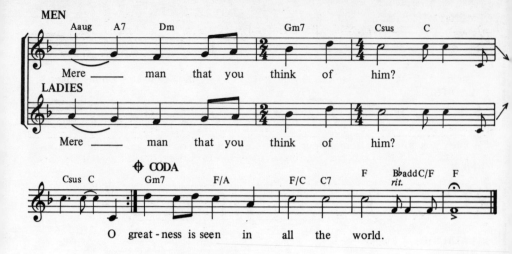

MEN

Aaug A7 Dm Gm7 Csus C

Mere ____ man that you think of him?

LADIES

Mere ____ man that you think of him?

CODA

Csus C Gm7 F/A F/C C7 F Bb add C/F F
rit.

O great-ness is seen in all the world.

7. Sing Praise To The Lord

Psalm 9 BOB FRASER

Steady

C Am7 Dm7 G7

I will praise you, Lord, with all my heart. I will

C Am7 3 Dm7 G7 3

tell of all ____ the won-der-ful things you've done. I ____ will

Em7 Am 3

sing with joy ____ be-cause ____ of you. ____ I will sing

D9 F/G G7

praise to you, ____ Al - migh - ty God, _____ sing

F G Am F

praise to the Lord, ____ sing praise to the Lord, ____ sing

9. I Will Sing To You

Psalm 13

SHEENA PECKHAM

10. Lord, Who May Enter Your Temple...?

Psalm 15

BOB FRASER

CHORUS

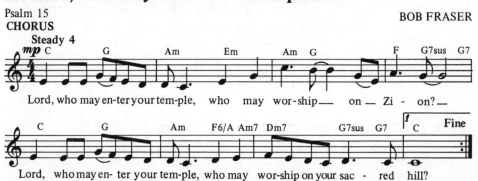

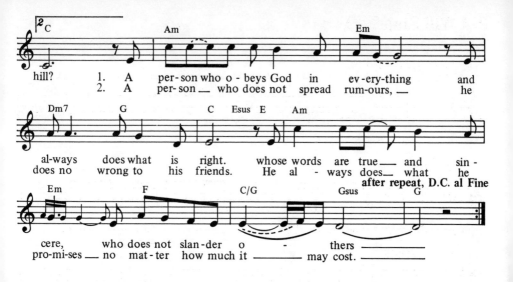

hill?

1. A per-son who o - beys God in ev -ery-thing and
2. A per-son __ who does not spread rum-ours, __ he

al-ways does what is right. whose words are true __ and sin -
does no wrong to his friends. He al - ways does __ what he

after repeat, D.C. al Fine

cere, who does not slan-der o - thers
pro-mi-ses __ no mat - ter how much it __ may cost.

11. I Love You, O Lord

Psalm 18

JOHN PANTRY

I love you, O Lord __ my __ strength, the Lord is my rock, my

Last time to Coda

for-tress and de - liv - erer, my God is the rock in whom I take shel - ter.

MEN **LADIES** **MEN**

My shield and sal - va-tion, My place __ of pro - tec - tion. I

LADIES **ALL**

love you, my Lord. O Lord, __ my __ strength. I love you, O

Lord __ my __ strength. {I call to the Lord, __ who is wor - thy of prai - ses, I
{I sing out your name _____ your praise a-mong the na-tions.

call to the Lord, who an-swers and saves __ me. Though
You are the rock, the source of sal-va-tion. And

death's cords en-tan-gle. He hears __ from His tem-ple. I called in dis-tress. He
who is this God? __ The King of ev-ery king-dom, whose word is the law be -

D.S. al ⊕ ⊕ CODA
ALL *rit.*

hears __ my __ voice, I whom I take shel - ter. __
fore Him who can stand.

12. The Law Of The Lord

Psalm 19   CHRISTOPHER NORTON

Gently, but rhythmically

The law of the Lord is per-fect, re-vi-ving the soul. __

__ The stat-utes of the Lord are trust-wor-thy, ma-king

wise __ the sim-ple. __ The pre-cepts of the Lord are

right, giv-ing joy to the heart. The com-mands of the Lord are

ra-diant giv-ing light to the eyes. The fear of the

Lord is pure, en-dur-ing for ev-er, the or-di-nan-ces of the Lord are sure and al-to-ge-ther right-eous. They are more pre-cious than gold, than much pure gold. they are sweet-er than ho-ney; than ho-ney from the comb.

13. The Heavens Declare

Psalm 19

BOB FRASER

Moderato

The hea-vens_ de-clare the glo-ry_ of God, the skies pro-claim the work of His hands. Their voice goes out in-to all the earth,_ their words to _ the ends of _ the world. _ The hea-vens _ de-clare the glo-ry, _____ the glo-ry of_ God. The hea-vens_ de-clare the glo-ry, _____ the glo-ry of_ God.

14. The Lord Is My Shepherd

Psalm 23

NORMAN WARREN

15. Fling Wide The Gates

Psalm 24

NORMAN WARREN

The Lord will bless them and save them. God will de-clare them
in-no-cent. Such are the peo-ple who come to God, who
come in-to the pre-sence of the God of Is-ra-el. Fling wide the gates
o-pen the an-cient doors, and the great king will come in. Fling wide the gates,
o-pen the an-cient doors, and the great king will come in.

16. Fling Wide The Gates

Psalm 24   BOB FRASER

Rhythmically

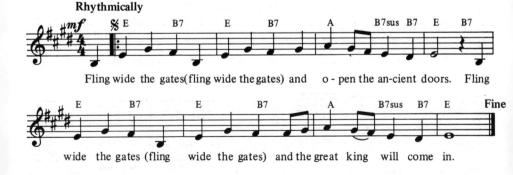

Fling wide the gates (fling wide the gates) and o-pen the an-cient doors. Fling
wide the gates (fling wide the gates) and the great king will come in.

1. Who is this great king? He is the Lord, strong and migh - ty.
2. Who is this great king? He made the world and all things in it.

1. Who is this great king? The Lord vic - tor - ious in bat - tle. Fling
2. Who is this great king? ____ He laid the world's foun-da - tions.

This psalm may be sung by employing an echo-effect in the refrain, between a solo voice and all.

17. Fling Wide The Gates

Psalm 24

DEREK HOWELL

CHORUS
Lively

Fling wide the gates. Op-en the an - cient doors and the great king will _ come

in. Fling wide the gates, o - pen the an - cient doors and the great king will come

in. ____ 1. The world and all ____ that is in it. are His be-cause He
2. Who has the right to go up to him En - ter - ing His
3. Who is this king so great and glor-ious, vic - tor ____ ious in

made it. He built the earth ____ on deep wa-ters, foun-
tem-ple On - ly the pure may come be - fore Him and
bat- tle? It is the Lord so strong and migh-ty, In

da - tions in the seas. ____ Fling wide the
they ____ shall be bless - ed. ____ Fling wide the
tri - umph see Him come. ____ Fling wide the

18. Teach Me Your Ways

Psalm 25

ERIC HEWITT

To you, O Lord, _____ I of - fer my prayer.

In you, my Lord, _____ I ___ trust. Save me

from the shame of de - feat, don't let my en - em - ies

___ gloat ov - er me. De - feat does not come to

those who trust in you, but to those who are

quick to re - bel a - gainst you.

19. The Lord Is My Light

Psalm 27

PHILIP WARREN

The Lord is my light and my sal - va - tion. I will fear __ no - one. __ The __ I have asked the Lord for one thing, one thing on - ly do I want to live in the Lord's house all my __ life. To mar - vel there at his good - ness. The

20. The Lord Is My Light

Psalm 27

SARAH LACY

The Lord is my light and my __ sal - va - tion __ I will __ fear no - one. The Lord pro - tects me from __ all __ dan - ger, __ I will ne - ver be a - fraid. 1. When

-ness in my life The Lord is my

⊕ CODA

- fraid.

21. Have Faith

Psalm 27

BOB FRASER

Flowing

1. The Lord is my light and sal - va - tion, I'll trust
2. Hear me Lord when I call to you, Have mer - cy and
3. Don't a - ban - don or leave me now, O Lord take

and o - bey. The Lord pro - tects me from
an - swer me. Teach me Lord what you
care of me. Lead me Lord a -

dan - ger, I'll ne - ver be a - fraid.
want me to do, And lead me in safe - ty.
long a safe path, Pro - tect me from en - e - mies.

CHORUS

Have faith, do not de - spair and trust in the

Lord. Have faith, do not de - spair and

trust in the Lord.

22. Ascribe To The Lord

Psalm 29

Moderato

BOB FRASER

23. Praise The Lord, You Heavenly Beings

Psalm 29
CHORUS

DEREK HOWELL

Praise the Lord, you hea-ven-ly be-ings, praise His glo-ry and power. Praise the glor-ious name of the Lord, bow ___ down be-fore the Ho-ly One, ___

VERSE

1. The voice of the Lord is heard on the seas. It ech-oes o-ver the o-cean. The voice of the Lord is ___ heard in might and maj-es-ty. The glor-ious God ___ thun-ders. ___

2. The voice of the Lord will shake the ___ trees, The migh-ty ce-dars of Le-ba-non. The voice of the Lord will ___ make the moun-tains leap like ___ calves and shake the de-sert pla-ces. ___

3. The voice of the Lord makes light-ning ___ flash, It strength-ens all his ___ peo-ple. The voice of the Lord brings ___ peace, O "Glo-ry to ___ God". He rules as King for ev-er. ___

D.C.

24. Lord, Your Constant Love

Psalm 36

NORMAN WARREN

ANTIPHON

Moderato

Lord, your con - stant love ____ rea - ches to the heavens, __ your faith - ful-

ness ____ ex - tends __ to the skies _____ your right - eous-ness is

tow - 'ring like the moun-tains _____ your jus - tice like the

depths __ of the sea. 1. How pre - cious O God is your con-stant love __
2. We feast on the food you pro-vide for us __

D.C.

__ we find pro - tec - tion in the sha - dow of your wings. __
__ you let us drink __ from the ri - ver of your good-ness.

25. Lord, You Put A New Song In My Mouth

Psalm 40

BOB FRASER

Lord, you put a new ____ song __ in my mouth

__ A hymn of praise to __ our __ God. __

Lord, you put a new ___ song ___ in my mouth, ___ a hymn of praise to our God. ___ Ma - ny ___ will see, ma - ny will fear, put their trust in ___ the Lord. ___ Ma - ny ___ will see, ma - ny will

Fine

D.S. al Fine

fear, put their trust in ___ the Lord. ___

26. May The Lord

Psalm 42

BOB FRASER

Gently

May the Lord show His con - stant love ___ dur - ing the day, ___ that I might have a song, ___ I might have a song ___ at night. ___ May the Lord show His con - stant love ___ dur - ing the day, ___ that I might have a prayer ___ to the God ___ of my life.

27. There Is A River

Psalm 46

BOB FRASER

CHORUS
With a strong beat

There is a ri-ver that brings joy to the ci-ty of God__

__ there is a ri-ver that brings joy to the ci-ty of God,__

__ God is in that ci - ty _____ and it will

ne - ver __ be de - stroyed. *Fine* Come and see what the Lord has__

done. See what a - ma - zing things He has done on__

earth. earth. _____

28. Clap Your Hands

Psalm 47

NORMAN WARREN

Brightly

LEADER

Clap your hands for joy,__ all __ peo - ple.

PEOPLE

C Em/B F/A C/G Dm/F G7 Csus C

Praise — God with loud — songs.

LEADER

Csus   C

The Lord the Most High is — to be feared.

Gm   Csus C

PEOPLE

C Em/B F/A C/G Dm/F G7 F/C C

Praise — God with loud — songs.

LEADER

C   Am Em/G Fmaj7 Dm7 G7sus G7

He is a great king rul-ing o-ver all the world.

PEOPLE

C G/B F/A C/G Dm/F G7 F/C C

Praise — God with loud — songs.

LEADER

C/Bb   Ab   Db/F G/F C/E Dm7

He gave us vic - tor - y o-ver the peo -ple.

PEOPLE

C Em7/B F/A C/E Dm G7 F/C C

Praise — God with loud — songs.

LEADER

C   Csus   Gm   Csus⁴₂ C

Sing praise to God, sing praise — to our King.

PEOPLE

C Em/B F/A C/G Dm/F G7 F/C C

Praise — God with loud — songs.

LEADER

C/Bb   Ab   Db/F G/F C/E Dm7

God is King o - ver all — the world.

PEOPLE

C Em7/B F/A C/E Dm G7 Am Am/G Fmaj7 G/F C/E Am Dm7 G7 C

ALL
Slower

rit. - - - - - - - - -

Praise — God with loud — songs.   Praise — God with loud — songs.

29. Create In Me

Psalm 51   CHRISTOPHER NORTON

Calmly

C   F

Cre - ate in — me — a pure heart O — God — and re-

new a stead-fast spi-rit with - in __ me. Cre - ate in __ me __ a pure

heart O __ God __ and re - new a stead-fast spi - rit with- in __ me   { Re -
                                                                       { Then

store to me the joy of your sal - va - tion, _____ and grant me a will - ing spi - rit
I will teach trans-gre - ssors your ways _____ and sin - ners will turn __ back __

to Fine last time

to sus - tain me. Cre-
to you.

30. The Sacrifices Of God

Psalm 51

BOB FRASER

The sac - ri - fi - ces of __ God are a bro - ken

spi-rit. __ A bro-ken and a con-trite heart, __ O God you will __ not de -

spise. The -spise.   *Fine*   Lord have mer - cy. Lord have

mer - cy,   Lord have mer - cy, Lord have mer - cy on me.

This Psalm may be sung as a round by combining **A** *and* **B**

31. I Will Give You Thanks

Psalm 63

NORMAN WARREN

32. Everything Shouts

Psalm 65

NORMAN WARREN

4. The pas - tures are filled with flocks, the _____ hill - sides are

to ANTIPHON

full of wheat.

LADIES

5. Ev-ery-thing shouts and sings for joy. Ev-ery-thing shouts and

MEN

5. Ev-ery-thing shouts and sings for joy _____

*Dm

C7sus C7 to ANTIPHON

LADIES

sings for joy. _____

MEN

sings for joy. _____

Optional division

33. May The People Praise You

Psalm 67

NORMAN WARREN

ANTIPHON

May the peo-ple praise you, O God; May the peo - ple

praise you. May the peo-ple praise you O God. May the peo - ple

34. Praise The Lord

Psalm 68

JOHN BARNARD

This item is intended for a solo voice with or without a choir. It may prove appropriate in congregational use, particularly for the sections beginning at B and D. The solo voice should sing the section at A.

35. Praise The Lord, The God Of Israel

Psalm 72

NORMAN WARREN

LEADER   PEOPLE

Praise the Lord, the God ___ of ___ Is - ra - el. Praise the Lord, the
God ___ of ___ Is - ra - el. He a - lone does these won-der-ful ___ things.

PEOPLE   LEADER

He a - lone does these won-der-ful things. Praise His glor - ious name for ev - er.

PEOPLE   LEADER

Praise His glor - ious name for ev - er. May his glo - ry fill the whole world.

PEOPLE   ALL

May his glo - ry fill the whole ___ world. A - men, A - - men.

36. May He Endure

Psalm 72

JOHN PANTRY

Brightly

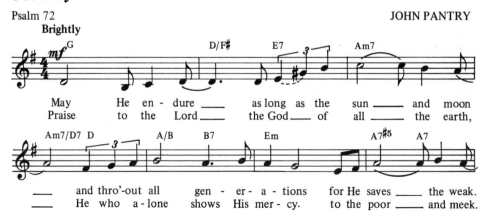

May He en - dure ___ as long as the sun ___ and moon
Praise to the Lord ___ the God ___ of all ___ the earth,

___ and thro'-out all gen - er - a - tions for He saves ___ the weak.
___ He who a - lone shows His mer - cy. to the poor ___ and meek.

Fresh as the rain _____ falls on the new _____ mown field _____
Kings shall bow down _____ and those _____ of no - ble birth _____

_____ all earth shall know _____ His bless - ing, _____ may He reign _____ in peace _____
_____ lay down their crowns _____ be - fore Him, _____ for He brings _____ them peace.

_____ All _____ na - tions, all _____ na - tions all _____ na - tions will be blessed.

_____ and they _____ will call _____ Him Lord. _____

_____ All _____

37. Start The Music

Psalm 81

DEREK HOWELL

Calypso style

CHORUS

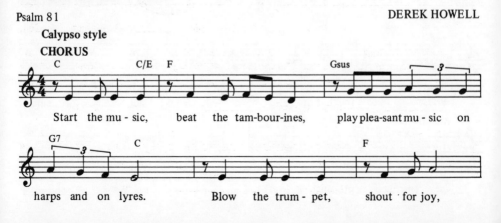

Start the mu - sic, beat the tam-bour-ines, play plea-sant mu - sic on

harps and on lyres. Blow the trum - pet, shout for joy,

Sing out your praise to the God of Ja - cob.
1. Lis - ten to what the
2. When in trou - ble to
3. I let you go on your

Lord would say
me you called
stub - born ways
I am the one who set you free.
Now I must say these words to you.
And still you do what - ev - er you please.

Let you lay down your loads of bricks,
I'm the Lord your God you see.
If you'd on - ly o - bey me,
took the bur - dens
You must not wor - ship
I would de - feat your

D. C. al Fine last time

off your backs.
a - ny but me.
en - e - mies.

38. Almighty God

Psalm 84

BOB FRASER

Oh how I love your tem - ple, Al - migh - ty God,
Al - migh - ty God. Oh how I love your
tem - ple. Al - migh - ty God, Al - migh - ty God.

For the Lord is our pro-tec-tor, ___ Glor-ious King, glor-ious King. Bless-ing us with kind-ness and ho-nour, ___ He does not re-fuse ___ an-y good thing. ___ O

D.C. al Fine

39. How Good It Is

Psalm 92

RICHARD PAIN

Israeli style

How good it is to give thanks to you ___ O Lord, to sing in your hon-our, O most High God. ___ to pro-claim your con-stant love ev-ery morn-ing and your faith-ful-ness ___ ev-ery night.

Fine

With the mu-sic of stringed in-stru-ments ___ and with me-lo-dy on the harp.

Your migh-ty deeds, O Lord, make me glad, — be-cause of what you have—

done. I sing for joy.

40. The Lord Is King

Psalm 93

NORMAN WARREN

ANTIPHON

The Lord is King, the Lord is King, He is clothed with ma-je-sty and

strength. The clothed with ma-je-sty and strength. 1. The earth is set

firm - ly in place and — can - not be —— moved.

to ANTIPHON

2. Your throne, O Lord has been firm from the be - gin - ning.

3. The o - cean depths raise their voice to the Lord: they

to ANTIPHON

raise their voice ____ and ____ roar.

4. The Lord rules su - preme ____ in ____ heav'n more

to ANTIPHON

pow - er - ful than waves of the sea.

41. Come Let Us Bow Down

Psalm 95

BOB FRASER

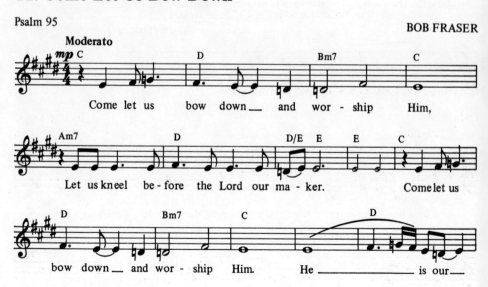

Come let us bow down ___ and wor - ship Him,

Let us kneel be - fore the Lord our ma - ker. Come let us

bow down ___ and wor - ship Him. He ____ is our ___

God. He _____ is our __ God.

We are the peo - ple __ He cares __ for __

the flock for which __ He pro - vides.

We are the peo - ple __ He cares __ for, __

the flock for which __ He pro - vides.

42. Come Let Us Praise The Lord

Psalm 95

BOB FRASER

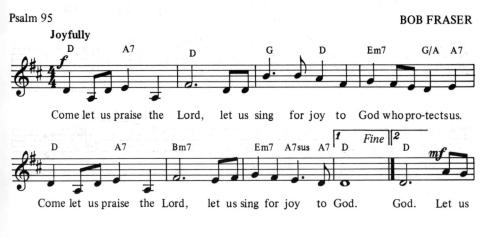

Come let us praise the Lord, let us sing for joy to God who pro-tects us.

Come let us praise the Lord, let us sing for joy to God. God. Let us

come be-fore_ Him with thanks-giv - ing and sing joy- ful songs of praise._ For the

D.C. al Fine

Lord is _ a migh - ty God, _ and migh-ty King _ ov - er all the gods. _

43. Sing A New Song

Psalm 98

NORMAN WARREN

LEADER/CHOIR (repeated by people)

Sing a new song to the Lord, he has done _ won-der-ful things.

By his own power and ho - ly strength. he has won _ the _ vic - tor - y.

Sing prai - ses to the _ Lord. Play _ mu - sic on the harps.

Blow _ trum-pets and _ horns and shout for joy _ to the Lord, our King.

ALL

and shout for joy _ to the Lord, our King. _

44. Shout For Joy To The Lord

Psalm 100

NORMAN WARREN

Shout for joy to the Lord, all the earth; serve the Lord with glad - ness!

Come be - fore him with joy - ful songs; give thanks to Him and praise His name. A - men.

45. Sing To The Lord, All The World

Psalm 100

NORMAN WARREN

CANTOR 1st time
PEOPLE 2nd time

Brightly

1. Sing to the Lord, all the world! Wor - ship the Lord with joy. Come be - fore him with hap-py songs! songs! Ne - ver for - get the Lord is God.

CANTOR   PEOPLE

God. He made us, He made us, and we be - long to him.

46. Sing To The Lord, All The World

Psalm 100

PHILIP WARREN

1. Sing to the Lord ____
   Wor-ship the Lord ____

____ all the world.   Come be -
____ with __ joy.

fore __ Him,   with hap-py songs.

Ac - know - ledge _____ that the Lord is God.   He
made us _____ and we be-long to Him.

we are His peo - ple,   we are His flock.

En-ter the tem - ple gates,   with thanks - giv - ing.

Go in- to its courts with praise, give thanks to Him and praise Him.

47. Praise The Lord, O My Soul

Psalm 104

NORMAN WARREN

ANTIPHON

Praise the Lord, my soul, Lord, how great you are.

Solo or Choir

Clothed with ma-jes-ty and glo-ry, praise the Lord, my soul __ 1. You

co-ver your-self with light. You spread out the heav-ens like a tent. You

to ANTIPHON

use the clouds as your cha-ri-ot, and ride on the wings of the wind.

2. You have set the earth so firm-ly, it shall not be moved.

to ANTIPHON

You have placed the o - cean ov-er it like a robe.

Slower

LADIES

3. You make springs flow in the

MEN   LADIES

vall-eys; ri-vers run bet-ween the hills. You send rain __ on the

MEN   **to ANTIPHON**

hills _____ And the earth is filled ___ with your bless - ings.

Lord, you have made so ma - ny things, how wise - ly you made them

all. The earth is filled with your crea - tures, they

to ANTIPHON

all de - pend on ___ you. I will sing to the

Lord all my life, as long as I live, I will sing prai-ses to my God.

May he be pleased —with my song. For my glad-ness comes from

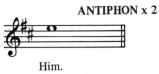

ANTIPHON x 2

Him.

48. From The East To The West

Psalm 113

BOB FRASER

Moderato

CHORUS

From the east to the west, from the east to the west praise the name of the Lord praise the name of the Lord The Lord rules ov - er all na - tions. From the na - tions. You ser - vants of the Lord praise His name. His name will be praised now and for ev - er. From the

CODA

49. Not To Us

Psalm 115

BOB FRASER

Not to us, O Lord, not to us, O Lord, but to your name be the

glo - ry. Not to us O Lord, not to us, O Lord, but to your name be the

glo - ry. The Lord re-mem-bers us and will bless us. He will bless the

house of Is - ra - el. He will bless those who fear the Lord, ____ both

small and great a - like. ____ Not to glo - ry. ____

50. Praise, Praise The Lord

Psalm 117

PAUL HERRINGTON

REFRAIN
Moderato

Praise _____ praise the Lord! Praise _____

____ Praise _____ the Lord. Praise _____ the Lord.

While choir sings 'ah' to refrain

SOLO

1. Praise ___ the Lord, ___ all ___ na - tions, praise ___

to REFRAIN

Him, ___ all ___ peo - ples.

SOLO

2. His love ___ for us ___ is ___ strong and His faith - ful -

to REFRAIN

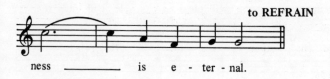

ness ___ is e - ter - nal.

51. Steadfast Love

Psalm 118

BOB FRASER

O give thanks to the Lord ___ for He is good, ___ for His love en - du - reth for ev - er. ___ O give ev - er ___ For His stead - fast love, His stead - fast love, His

love en-du-reth for ev-er. _____ For His ev-er. _____

_____ O give O give thanks to the Lord _____ of Lords _____

_____ for His love en-du-reth for ev-er. _____ O give

ev-er. _____ For His stead-fast love, His stead-fast

love, His love en-du-reth for ev-er. _____ For His

stead-fast love, His stead-fast love, His love en-

du-reth for ev-er. _____ For His

52. Your Word, O Lord

Psalm 119   CHRISTOPHER NORTON

Your word O Lord will last for-ev-er, it is e-ter-nal in

hea-ven. Your faith-ful-ness en - dures thro' all a - ges.

You have set the earth in place and it re - mains. _____

place and it re - mains. How I love your law, I think a - bout it all day

long. ___ Your word is a lamp to guide me and a light for my

path. place and it re - mains.

53. Show Me

Psalm 119

ROGER MAYOR

Show me ___ how much you love me Lord ___ and

save me ___ ac-cor-ding to your pro - mise. Show me ___ how much you

love me Lord ___ and save me ___ ac-cor-ding to your pro - mise.

CHOIR

Teach me Lord __ the mean-ing of __ your laws

D. %̸ al Fine

and I will o - bey them at all __ times.

54. Happy Are Those

Psalm 119   ERIC HEWITT

Hap - py are __ those whose lives are fault-less, who live ac -

cord - ing to the law of the Lord. Hap -py are __ those who

fol - low his com - mands, who o - bey him with all their heart. __

__ They ne - ver do wrong; __ they walk in the Lord's ways.

Lord, you have gi - ven us your laws and told us to o - bey them faith-ful -

ly. __ How I hope that I shall be faith - ful in

keep - ing your in - struct - - tions. If I pay at -

ten - tion to all your com-mands, then I will not be put to shame.

As I learn your right-eous judge-ments, I will praise you with a pure heart.

Slower

I will o - bey your laws, Ne - ver a -

ban - don me!

55. I Was Glad

Psalm 122

NORMAN WARREN

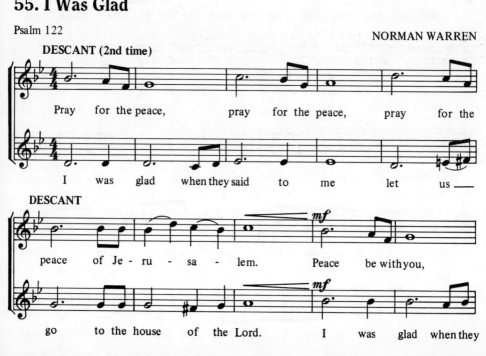

DESCANT (2nd time)

Pray for the peace, pray for the peace, pray for the

I was glad when they said to me let us

DESCANT

peace of Je - ru - sa - lem. Peace be with you,

go to the house of the Lord. I was glad when they

DESCANT

peace be with you, peace be with you, peace be with

said to me let us ___ go to the house ___ of the

DESCANT

you. you.

Lord. Lord.

56. Lord I Look Up To You

Psalm 123

NORMAN WARREN

ANTIPHON
Gently

Lord, I look up to you, up to hea - ven where you rule.

Lord, I look up to you, up to hea - ven where you rule.

MEN
Unison ... **WOMEN**

As a ser - vant de-pends on his mas - ter, as a maid de - pends on her

D.C. to ANTIPHON ... **WOMEN**

Dsus D MEN Unison

mis - tress. So we will keep look-ing to ___ you, O Lord our ___

ALL ... **D.C. to ANTIPHON**

God un - til you have mer - cy on us.

57. What If The Lord

NORMAN WARREN

Psalm 124

REFRAIN (Men)

What if the Lord ___ had not been on ___ our ___ side? An - swer, O Is - ra - el!

VERSE (Ladies)

If the Lord had ___ not been on our side,
Then the flood would have car-ried us a - way,

When our e - ne-mies at -
the wa-ter would have

tacked us,
cov-ered us.

Then they would have swall-owed us a - live ___
The ___ rag - ing tor - rent would have drowned us.

to REFRAIN

in their fur - ious ___ an - ger a - gainst us.
Let us thank the Lord, ___ let us thank the Lord. ___

LADIES

La - la - la - la - la - la - la - la - la, la - la - la - la - la - la

MEN

Our help comes from ___ the ___ Lord, who made hea-ven and

la - la.   La - la - la - la - la - la - la - la - la.

MEN

earth.   Our   help   comes   from___ the ___Lord.

LADIES

La - la - la - la - la - la,   la - la - la - la - la.

MEN

Who   made   hea - ven and   earth.

58. When The Lord Brought Us Back

Psalm 126

NORMAN WARREN

Brightly
CANTOR

When the   Lord brought us   back from Je - ru - sa - lem,   it   was   like   a ___

REFRAIN (People)

dream.   How   we laughed, how we sang   for ___ joy ___   It   was   like   a ___

CANTOR

dream!   It   was like ___ a ___ dream!   Then the oth - er   na - tions

to REFRAIN

said   a - bout ___ us   "The ___ Lord   did   great   things for   us."

In - deed he did great_ things for us. how ____ hap-py we were.
Let those who wept as they sowed their seed, ga-ther the har-vest with joy.

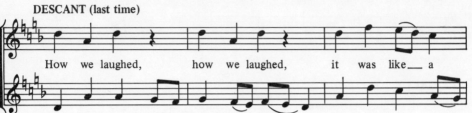

DESCANT (last time)

How we laughed,   how we laughed,   it was like_ a

How we laughed, how we sang for joy.____ It was like a ____

DESCANT

dream. ____ It was like ____ a ____ dream!

dream. _____ It was like ____ a __ dream!

59. Unless The Lord

Psalm 127   ANDREW MARIES

Gently but rhythmically

Un - less the Lord _____ build _ the house _____ Un-

less the Lord _____ build _ the house __   Its

build - ers, _ its build - ers la - bour in vain. Un- vain, _____

__ they la - bour in vain. _____

60. O Israel Put Your Trust In The Lord

Psalm 130

BOB FRASER

O Is - ra - el, _____ put your hope in the Lord, ___ O

Is - ra - el, __ put your hope in the Lord __ for with the Lord __ is un -

fail - ing love __ and with Him is full re - demp - tion _____ O

- tion. __ I wait for the Lord _____ I wait for the Lord

My soul waits and in His word I put my hope. O

61. Out Of The Depths

Psalm 130

ANDREW MARIES

Out of the depths I cry to you O ___

Lord. O Lord, hear my cry. Out of the depths I cry to you, O ___

Lord, O Lord hear my cry. _____ 1. If you kept a note of my sins, _____ O Lord who could stand? But there is for- give - ness with you, _____ there-fore you are feared. Out of the _____ 2. I wait for the Lord _____ and on _____ his word put my trust _____ my soul _____ waits for _____ the Lord. More than watch - men wait _____ for _____ the morn - ing. _____ —3. Put your trust in the Lord _____ for with the Lord is un - fail - ing love _____ and with him _____ is full _____ re - demp - tion, Hope in the Lord. _____ cry.

62. A Prayer Of Humble Trust

Psalm 131

NORMAN WARREN

ANTIPHON

We will trust in the Lord, now and for ev - er.

SOLO

now and for ev - er. 1. Lord, I have giv-en up my pride and

to ANTIPHON

turned a - way, turned a - way from my ar - ro - gance.

2. In - stead I am con - tent and at peace, ____ as a child ____ lies

rall.

quiet - ly in its moth - er's arms. So my heart, so my heart is

a tempo

quiet with - in. ____ We will trust in the Lord, ____ now and for

ev - er, now and for ev - er.

63. How Good And Pleasant

Psalm 133

BOB FRASER

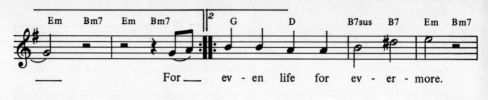

For — ev - en life for ev - er - more.

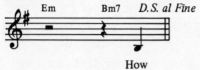

How

64. Come Praise The Lord

Psalm 134

DON SCULLY

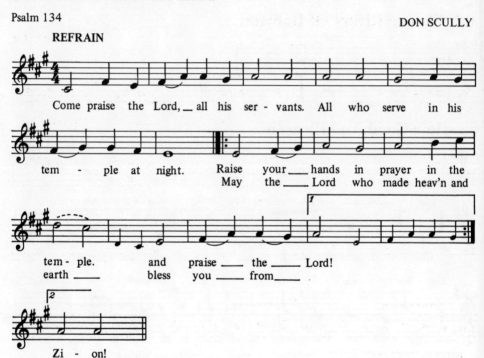

REFRAIN

Come praise the Lord, — all his ser - vants. All who serve in his

tem - ple at night. Raise your — hands in prayer in the
May the — Lord who made heav'n and

tem - ple. and praise — the — Lord!
earth — bless you — from —

Zi - on!

65. Come Praise The Lord

Psalm 134

BOB FRASER

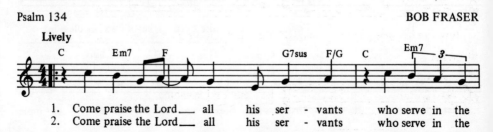

Lively

1. Come praise the Lord — all his ser - vants who serve in the
2. Come praise the Lord — all his ser - vants who serve in the

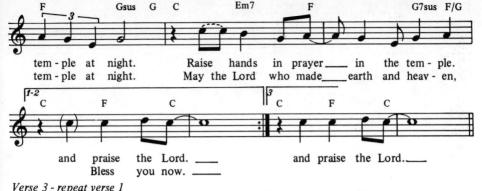

tem - ple at night. Raise hands in prayer____ in the tem - ple.
tem - ple at night. May the Lord who made____ earth and heav - en,

and praise the Lord. ____ and praise the Lord.____
Bless you now. _____

Verse 3 - repeat verse 1

66. By The Rivers Of Babylon

Psalm 137

BOB FRASER

Gently

By the ri - vers of Ba - by - lon, _____ by the ri - vers of

Ba - by - lon, _____ we sat and wept.__ when we re - mem - ber'd Zi -

- on. By the ri - vers of How can we sing____ the

songs of the Lord? __ How can we sing ____ the songs of the Lord?__

How can we sing __ the songs of the Lord,__ while in a fo - reign land?

⊕ **CODA**

rit. - - - - - - - - - - -

A and B combine

- on. _____

67. By The Waters Of Babylon

Psalm 137

ANDREW MARIES

By the wa-ters of Ba-by-lon _____ we sat and _ wept,

when we re - mem - bered _____ Zi - on.

Fine

1. There in the pop - lars, _____ we _ hung our harps
2. How can we sing the Lord's song in a fo - riegn land?

For there our cap - tors asked for songs _____ They said:
If I for - get you O Je - ru - sa-lem, May my

"Sing us one of the songs of Zi - on." _____
right - hand for - get its skill. _____

after v. 2 D.C. al Fine

68. I Will Praise You

Psalm 138

BOB FRASER

Joyfully

I will praise you, O Lord _ with all _ my heart I will

to Coda

praise you O Lord _ with all _ my heart. I will

bow down to - wards your ho - ly tem - ple _____ I will praise your

name for your love and faith - ful - ness. _____ I will praise you, O Lord

_____ I will praise you O Lord _____ with all _____ my heart

I will praise you, O Lord _____ with all _____ my heart.

I will praise your name for your love and faith - ful - ness. _____

CODA

_____ I will praise.

69. Praise The Lord

Psalm 146

NORMAN WARREN

Praise _____ the

Lord. _____ Praise the Lord _ my _ soul _____ I will praise

CHORUS

him. _____ as _ long _ as I live _____ I _ will

sing, I will sing to my God all my life. Praise ___ the
Lord. ___ Praise the Lord, _ my ___ soul. soul.

70. Praise The Lord

NORMAN WARREN

Psalm 148

Praise the Lord. Praise the Lord from
hea - ven, Praise the Lord from hea - ven. You that live in the
heights a - bove, you that live in the heights a-bove. Praise him, all his
an - gels, praise him, all his an - gels. All his heav-en -ly
arm - ies. All his heav-en-ly arm - ies. Praise him, sun and
moon, ___ praise him, sun and moon.___ Praise him ___ shin - ing stars
praise him ___ shin - ing stars. Praise him, high - est hea - vens,

name — of the Lord.   Let   them   all   praise the   name — of the Lord.

ALL
Maestoso

Let   them   all   praise the   name — of the Lord.

71. Praise The Lord

Psalm 149   NORMAN WARREN

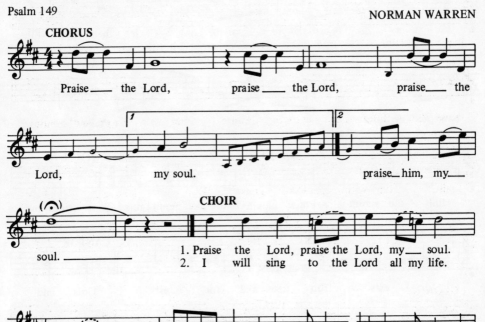

CHORUS

Praise —— the Lord,   praise —— the Lord,   praise—— the

Lord,   my soul.   praise— him, my —

soul. —————   **CHOIR**

1. Praise   the   Lord, praise the Lord, my — soul.
2. I   will   sing   to   the   Lord   all   my   life.

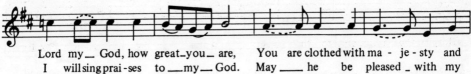

Lord my — God, how great—you— are,   You are clothed with ma - je - sty and
I   will sing prai - ses   to —my — God.   May —— he   be   pleased — with my

D.C.

glo - ry. ————
song. ————

72. Praise God In His Temple

Psalm 150

C. V. STANFORD

ALL

Praise God in His tem - ple. Praise His strength __ in ____ heaven.

Praise Him for the mighty things He has done. __ Praise His su - preme __ greatness.

Praise Him with trum - pets. Praise Him with the harps and lyres.

ALL

Praise Him with drums and danc - ing. Praise Him with harps and flutes.

MEN

Praise Him with cym - bals: Praise Him with loud ____ cymbals.

ALL

Praise the Lord all liv - ing crea - tures: Praise _____ the Lord. _____

GLORIA

Glory to the Father, and to the Son: __ And to the Ho - ly Spirit;

As it was in the beginning, is now and ev - er shall be: world without end. __

A - - - - men.

73. Praise The Lord

Psalm 150

LEE ABBEY

Praise the Lord, ___ praise Him in his tem - ple! Praise Him for the ___ migh - ty things, he ___ has ___ done. Praise the Lord! ___ Praise Him for His great - ness. Praise Him with trum - pets, harps and lyres. All liv - ing crea - tures praise. O praise, O praise, praise the Lord! _____

74. Praise God In His Temple

Psalm 150

DEREK HOWELL

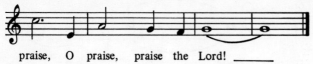

Praise God ___ in His tem - ple. Praise His strength in heav'n. Praise His great - ness ___ and the migh-ty things ___ He's

done.   done.   Praise   Him with {trum - pet. / tam - bou-rine. / dan - cing.

Praise   Him   with {harp / flute / drum   Praise

Him   with cym - bals,   loud cym - bals   If you're breath-ing,

Praise _____ the Lord. _____

ACKNOWLEDGEMENTS

The publishers wish to express their thanks to the following for permission to reproduce the following in this book:

Boosey & Hawkes Music Publishers Ltd, 295 Regent Street, London, W1R 8JH for *Almighty God* by Bob Fraser; *Answer me* by Christopher Norton; *Ascribe to the Lord* by Bob Fraser; *By the rivers of Babylon* by Bob Fraser; *Come, let us bow down* by Bob Fraser; *Come, let us praise* by Bob Fraser; *Come, praise the Lord* by Bob Fraser; *Create in me* by Christopher Norton; *Fling wide the gates* by Bob Fraser; *Fling wide the gates* by Derek Howell; *From the east* by Bob Fraser; *Have faith* by Bob Fraser; *How good and pleasant* by Bob Fraser; *I call to the Lord for help* by Christopher Norton; *I will praise you* by Bob Fraser; *Listen to my words, O Lord* by Christopher Norton; *Lord, who may enter* by Bob Fraser; *Lord, you put a new song* by Bob Fraser; *May the Lord* by Bob Fraser; *Not to us* by Bob Fraser; *O Israel put your hope* by Bob Fraser; *Praise God in his temple* by Derek Howell; *Praise the Lord* by Derek Howell; *Sing praise to the Lord* by Bob Fraser; *Start the music* by Derek Howell; *Steadfast love* by Bob Fraser; *The heavens declare* by Bob Fraser; *The law of the Lord* by Christopher Norton; *The Lord is my light* by Sarah Lacy; *The sacrifices of God* by Bob Fraser; *There is a river* by Bob Fraser; *Your word, O Lord* by Christopher Norton. Copyright 1989 and 1990 by Ears and Eyes Music, reprinted by permission of Boosey and Hawkes Music Publishers Ltd.

Hodder & Stoughton Ltd, 47 Bedford Square, London, WC1B 3DP for extracts from the *New International Version* of the Bible. Copyright 1973, 1978, 1984 by International Bible Society.

Jubilate Hymns Ltd, The Vicarage, Tonbridge, Kent, TN9 1HD for *A prayer of humble trust* by Norman Warren; *Clap your hands* by Norman Warren; *Everything shouts* by Norman Warren; *Fling wide the gates* by Norman Warren; *I was glad* by Norman Warren; *I will give you thanks* by Norman Warren; *Listen to my words, O Lord* by Norman Warren; *Lord, I look up to you* by Norman Warren; *Lord, your constant love* by Norman Warren; *May the people praise you* by Norman Warren; *Praise the Lord* by John Barnard; *Praise the Lord* by Norman Warren; *Praise the Lord, O my soul* by Norman Warren; *Shout for joy to the Lord* by Norman Warren; *Sing a new song* by Norman Warren; *Sing to the Lord* by Norman Warren; *The Lord is King* by Norman Warren; *The Lord is my shepherd* by Norman Warren; *What if the Lord* by Norman Warren; *When I lie down* by Norman Warren; *When the Lord brought us back* by Norman Warren. Copyright 1991 by John Barnard, Norman Warren and Jubilate Hymns Ltd.

Andrew Maries, St Michael Le Belfry, York for *By the waters of Babylon* by Andrew Maries; *Out of the depths* by Andrew Maries; *Unless the Lord* by Andrew Maries. Copyright 1991 by Andrew Maries.

John Pantry for *I love you, O Lord* by John Pantry; *May he endure* by John Pantry. Copyright 1991 by John Pantry.

All other works in this collection, including the compilation, are Copyright by the British and Foreign Bible Society, Stonehill Green, Westlea, Swindon, SN5 7DG.

None of the works in this collection may be reproduced in any form without the written permission of the copyright holder.

Index

Title	Composer	Psalm	No
A prayer of humble trust	*Norman Warren*	131	62
Almighty God	*Bob Fraser*	84	38
Answer me	*Christopher Norton*	4	3
Ascribe to the Lord	*Bob Fraser*	29	22
By the rivers of Babylon	*Bob Fraser*	137	66
By the waters of Babylon	*Andrew Maries*	137	67
Clap your hands	*Norman Warren*	47	28
Come, let us bow down	*Bob Fraser*	95	41
Come, let us praise	*Bob Fraser*	95	42
Come, praise the Lord	*Bob Fraser*	134	65
Come, praise the Lord	*Don Scully*	134	64
Create in me	*Christopher Norton*	51	29
Everything shouts	*Norman Warren*	65	32
Fling wide the gates	*Bob Fraser*	24	16
Fling wide the gates	*Derek Howell*	24	17
Fling wide the gates	*Norman Warren*	24	15
From the east	*Bob Fraser*	113	48
Happy are those	*Eric Hewitt*	119	54
Have faith	*Bob Fraser*	27	21
How good and pleasant	*Bob Fraser*	133	63
How good it is	*Richard Pain*	92	39
How much longer?	*Philip Warren*	13	8
I call to the Lord for help	*Christopher Norton*	3	1
I love you, O Lord	*John Pantry*	18	11
I was glad	*Norman Warren*	122	55
I will give you thanks	*Norman Warren*	63	31
I will praise you	*Bob Fraser*	138	68
I will sing to you	*Sheena Peckham*	13	9
Listen to my words, O Lord	*Christopher Norton*	5	4
Listen to my words, O Lord	*Norman Warren*	5	5
Lord, I look up to you	*Norman Warren*	123	56
Lord, who may enter	*Bob Fraser*	15	10
Lord, you put a new song	*Bob Fraser*	40	25
Lord, your constant love	*Norman Warren*	36	24
May he endure	*John Pantry*	72	36
May the Lord	*Bob Fraser*	42	26
May the people praise you	*Norman Warren*	67	33
Not to us	*Bob Fraser*	115	49
O Israel put your hope	*Bob Fraser*	130	60
O Lord, our Lord	*David French*	8	6
Out of the depths	*Andrew Maries*	130	61

Praise God in his temple	C V Stanford	150	72
Praise God in his temple	Derek Howell	150	74
Praise the Lord	Derek Howell	29	23
Praise the Lord	John Barnard	68	34
Praise the Lord	Lee Abbey	150	73
Praise the Lord	Norman Warren	72	35
Praise the Lord	Norman Warren	146	69
Praise the Lord	Norman Warren	148	70
Praise the Lord	Norman Warren	149	71
Praise the Lord, O my soul	Norman Warren	104	47
Praise, praise the Lord	Paul Herrington	117	50
Shout for joy to the Lord	Norman Warren	100	44
Show me	Roger Mayor	119	53
Sing a new song	Norman Warren	98	43
Sing praise to the Lord	Bob Fraser	9	7
Sing to the Lord	Norman Warren	100	45
Sing to the Lord	Philip Warren	100	46
Start the music	Derek Howell	81	37
Steadfast love	Bob Fraser	118	51
Teach me your ways	Eric Hewitt	25	18
The heavens declare	Bob Fraser	19	13
The Law of the Lord	Christopher Norton	19	12
The Lord is king	Norman Warren	93	40
The Lord is my light	Philip Warren	27	19
The Lord is my light	Sarah Lacy	27	20
The Lord is my shepherd	Norman Warren	23	14
The sacrifices of God	Bob Fraser	51	30
There is a river	Bob Fraser	46	27
Unless the Lord	Andrew Maries	127	59
What if the Lord?	Norman Warren	124	57
When I lie down	Norman Warren	4	2
When the Lord brought us back	Norman Warren	126	58
Your word, O Lord	Christopher Norton	119	52